CU00949697

ASYLUM

ASYLUM

Sean Borodale

CAPE POETRY

1 3 5 7 9 10 8 6 4 2

Jonathan Cape, an imprint of Vintage,
20 Vauxhall Bridge Road,
London SW1V 2SA

Jonathan Cape is part of the Penguin Random House group of companies
whose addresses can be found at global.penguinrandomhouse.com

Copyright © Sean Borodale 2018

Sean Borodale has asserted his right to be identified as the
author of this Work in accordance with the Copyright, Designs
and Patents Act 1988

First published by Jonathan Cape in 2018

penguin.co.uk/vintage

A CIP catalogue record for this book is available
from the British Library

ISBN 9781911214021

Typeset in 11/13 pt Bembo by Jouve (UK), Milton Keynes
Printed and bound in Great Britain by TJ International Ltd, Padstow, Cornwall

Penguin Random House is committed to a sustainable future for
our business, our readers and our planet. This book is made
from Forest Stewardship Council® certified paper.

for Orlando and Louis

ANTIGONE: *Speak, for you are reaching the last extremity*

Sophocles, *Oedipus at Colonus*

CONTENTS

ASYLUM

REHEARSAL AT ST CUTHBERT'S SWALLET

What is this odd sensation?

Why do I feel more invisible, mere memory
as I dip under stone?

Having entered the swallet,
having dammed up the stream,
how do I blind my way in, and touch,
bridge my way down with knees on one side?

Isn't this odd;
heels pressing the vertical dark

going down out of attention
from the thin world of the bubble of air;
the gleaming skull's sutures,
its crown whispering.

Why do I feel more dark,
out of the sights of any bird, the sounds also?

Why do I prevail in emptiness,
cut from the tension of speed and appetite;
carrying this odd death with me down

under roads like spears scattered across miles?

Why do I have to forget what I love;
carrying its core in an urn of sound?

Why do I have to go on
slithering out of the lit Anthrocene, like this;
to slough off the sun, its cadence of distance;
with my hunt for the answers, my lit skin,
all it is now: the last collapsed tunnel?

Why am I buried in close-fitting rock?
Am I insured? I may have forgotten.

SKELETAL ELEMENTS OF
A WOMAN SURFACING
FROM A GRAVE-PLOT
AT STANTON DREW

It comes to light,
walking over the grass, kicking molehills
with that sense: *they know more.*

The seclusion, look around at it:
topsoil, subsoil, below that, the water line;
below that, the depth of persistence out of every storm;
long plots of burial.

Uphill in the churchyard,
bright heaps of heavy red soil;
the grass, thin.

Each of us fixedly developing our own thoughts,
tilting horizons to the churchyard earth.

The long double-roots of teeth –
canine, incisor;
the scatter of rib bones, arm bones.

They could not have forecast: glancing back at them,
her relatives' faces dredging a hole's spare form,
lowering a Plenty Price.

Glancing back: they could not have foreseen
the wash of her litter; bones like wave-spume
drifting up discharged and naked,
like anthers of flowers.

Her pieces, here, scaring the now.
Her panoply, lit:
her post-self's inner furniture
like broken chairs between black graveyard yews;
dipping their red wood
into the same bother of planting,
same publishing of headstones; the same marked plots
which have erupted their principle of eternal sleep,
risen as flamed out of burial and gone awry,
wreaking jigsaws of havoc.

The brief order of a corpse
stapled in with sods and soil weight.

The coffins must have been soft, you say.
They must have been soft coffins.

Curved porcelain-cup pieces of brain-mantle.
Her ordinary skull broken at every suture.
Her yellows porous.

Teeth and vertebrae on tumbled-up soil;
of Hannah Plenty Price, teeth that still shine.

The spongy hard crust of a bone
mealy with fragments;
the fractured littering
through oxide, blood-coloured, heavy-clay earth.

The whole yard is lifting its burial;
the sun
hinging its inhumations
into the spill of the everyday.

The whole place
a broken mouth of loose teeth.

4

Roots
dipping and drawing the flesh of the shade;
like sherbet
you taste in your mouth

as we drive
south, back to the higher hills.

VOICE OF AN ARCHAEOLOGIST AT PRIDDY NINE MAIDENS (TO WEAVE RESPONSES INTO WHEN THE WIND BLOWS, AND THE VOICE STARTS UP)

I come to lament.

My words trail off
into low, hushed statements at the verge of sound.

Earthen, the mound. Burial, pregnant.
A she, of contents exposed.
I feel a.
Wreck.

Maybe she died in childbirth
and the pelvis had been removed with the foetus.

Beads of amber, faience, jet, shale, a copper awl.
A kind of dress fastening.

A woman today.
This.
Who excavated the richest burial on the Mendip.

Under bleak wind, she speaks into soil.

It came from our voices
blowing this way between the outposts of our working;
scraping back air,
seeing the scarred detail in relief.

And we surmised: turfs from outlying regions.
I feel a.
Wreck.

Is that the transparency of people?
Is that them now,
taking a part in the burial; bringing the sods;

far off, on the wind-line cutting this way?

REHEARSAL AT
WATERWHEEL SWALLET

A waterwheel
jammed in the socket of its mouth;

its dry throat sings nothing
but a draught of depth.

Black walls.
Lead ore, called galena.

A ventricle of scored-out crevasse
dissolved into petrified sea floors.

From here, a ladder unravels
into splash;

a black lake twenty feet deep,
its scab of gleam in the mist.

At breath's temperature,
fragments of lung
aerosol the light beam, at depth.

Lagoon of infill
sinking with deadweight;
a bladder of lamp black.

I hang
hearing its hall-of-sound mirror
the breathing self.

The weight of life's winding lurches
infinitely down on its lug of fall.

And so on,
into the long-case of the earth.

EASTWATER
CAVERN VOICE-TEST

It is almost a passion, the gloom;
bodies, only extravagances of air,
so still, leeched-out
and rich with slumber.

It is almost a mineral, the waste;
gothic, deep and dreadful –
there, that appointed word
which corners the voice:
Dread.

Almost a snuff, the red paste earth,
almost acoustic
pressing the voice back into the blackness of the throat;

muffling, before it steadies;
absorbed
into dry, scaly galleries of rock;
ruptured, torn into deeper fathoms.

Terms such as 'bedding plane'
do nothing to obscure the illness of the place.

A rough, dry decline;
so thin after that, so weak and variable.

The only route: to drop deeper, irreversible.
Lie at a gruesome end
as a heap in a heap,
the instrument of the bones.

So strangely wooden;
so curled and dismantled. Shrunken;

something a pilgrim would smooth with his feet.

BEACON HILL INHUMATION
(RE-BURIED WOMAN)

They put her in the ground
where white moths complicate the evening

under trees where it is dark.
They might have murdered her.

There is little mercy
in the syndrome of the living.

Her indented present:
airless, mothless.

A SMALL HOVEL INSIDE THE
SELF, EASTWATER CAVERN

Nothing has come here
that is more than flicker,
that has not brought
the bright, hurt language of its sun.

It took this stalactite
longer to grow than any nation.

A hatch into the unlit:
under-rooms, under-fields.
Like dry leaves in a hole,
bits of me sit.

An odd interior taxidermy;
dead space;
or space so slowly living
it does not cede time;

but an assailing language,
that assails me like falling water;
a discipline
of decline.

EARTHWORM

Impossible to register
        what worms do under the footprint

without digging up the long voices of them
  casting dead miles into potent food

eating lines in the life of the dark
        tubular   single-minded   all of them

one writing single mind of multiplicity
        touching sides to mate

        a worm-parent frayed to millions
totally sensed   but blind

 blindly feeling along tunnels below horizons
bleeding through patches of the soil's skull.

AVELINE'S HOLE

The red paste earth
almost acoustic,
pressing the voice
back into the blackness of the throat.

The red paste earth
almost acoustic,
pressing the voice
back into the blackness of the throat.

The red paste earth
almost acoustic,
pressing the voice
back into the blackness of the throat.

PICKING THROUGH THE RUINS OF FUSSELL IRONWORKS ALONG THE LOWER MELLS STREAM

For those who need the black hole,
the pondering collapse, the pending flood:
I come to pay homage.

Nearly impossible to say what I look for,
walking fast through trees,
seeing for the malevolent.

Moss drips;
the foot moves over stale mud.

The river's vague speed
absorbs the interest of the suicide
inside every body.

Iron-oxide.
Colloids of fox-fur-red clay
bleed out of riverbanks.

Every voice is potent in the air's moisture,
erased individuals;

a collapsing, slow mass of damp and stone
into the cavities of rooms.

Hard to see anything
devoid of failing, damp light.

The time-zone weirds of the ruin invite me:
stalactites
into previous, vast furnace ovens;

bodies gone that had arranged fire
so controlled it was highly expressive:
in one concentration,
enough to melt iron.

Walls of slag-blocks, of vitreous waste.

Defiant, to be quick-living, to talk at all.
Should be stalactite, would be best,
leaking slowly through the fall of years.

Or be still,
letting the flow of water
agitate stone
only particles at a time.

How can speech be unlaboured;
a single word issue
at the rate of stone, out of rock;

to be alone,
with the population of collapsing drips
as they flash apart;
with no sight, no hearing, no shallow breath;

feeling the blurs of earth, feeling the bleb grow
swelling water full of its milky stone.

There are no working men,
no onerous words or ledgers;
none killing their babies of iron.
Babies like ingots:
faceless, mouthless, eyeless, fingerless, toeless.

The odd, lumpy work-table frame of iron
is cast askew;

the odd track of narrow-gauge iron-work rail
is damaged in situ.

I asked for leniency: I got these woods.
Their sodden mouldy ground; their soft iron memory
staining
subsoil without me.

RESPONSE TO FINDING A FOSSILISED FERN AT WRITHLINGTON COAL BATCHES NEAR RADSTOCK

Time not as we know it;
but another time quite skilled in losing things.

Time pressed flat in a thousand directions
the fern's delicate gap resists.

A small leaf-sleeve of paper,
a message meaning nothing.
A small cough in the brittle stillness
of earth floating on rock.

A mere bent bit of triumph resisting
the weight of billions of tonnes of death
carpeting a drowned wet bog. A drowned dead mineral
crushed under the felting and pressure
of another forest under another horizon
so vast
it has forgotten it is curved,
connected to every second of this Earth.

A fern made of matter;
a split-second of consciousness gone into seeing.
Seeing what the beauty shines with;

the queer entity of its coffin
split like a nutshell,
in the hand of a five-year-old child
taking time off from school.

We heard it crack like a collar-bone hitting the floor.

Better than it was
fluttering in the bright mid-morning air of a young day.
Waterless and lightless, virtually free.

FOSSILISED FERN COMPRESSION

It is precisely cut like the insides of a watch
which counts nothing, serves nothing, wastes nothing.

The rest is the black torpor of unsung carbon.

This batch, this spoil heap
used by boys for bike-tracks.
Rubbish-heap testimony: a black glitter

of broken TVs, Bakelite phones,
fire grates, old men
in armchairs jammed among ashtrays,
their lungs breathing on in captivity,
their expressions printing
to the hardening festoon of a grave.

The hand deep in its pocket
fumbling for a key, just paused.
A key whose jagged shape
is copied from the parent of all keys.

And then,
the negative brilliance of a minute detail
would come to rest,
finally, for long enough
to disturb its ancient dreaming:
for access to value;

a value so tiny,
so briefly mistaken for an answer
to the cold and the dark;
abstract and flapping its gritty feathers in the fire,

to get to the light,
to sit by the blaze, to hear the story tell its ends;
terrible and ancient,
and weak, so weak;

staring by the warmth, saying, *it was better*,
by the virtual fact of its knowledge,
better too than it was before this, much better.

MEASURING THE EFFECT OF DARKNESS ON THE VOICE FOR 30 MINUTES, GOATCHURCH CAVERN

i

I bring fear of the dark,
a length of rope, an abject desire.
I footstep whispers, its damp;
stairs oozing me through pooled vapour,
the hole.

Some may see light fraying off over the threshold
into its fissure.
Bats whirr.

The voice in its cavity, intuit its depth
by speech, strangeness; the echo frays.
Many, many
voices boom up randomly.

I strike a match – lightening the dark sound.

A sulphurous yellow
slithers along matchwood and fails,
congealing shadow
through the stone of Burrington Combe.

ii

I exist in stone the colour of grey.
Grey with nursed, small incidents;
pre-born, growing hair from stone.

A fabric over my face;
a blankness, deadness
weirdly contrives to exist.

I am being as still as I can:
devoid of light, I walk on the ruin
over the boulder, the slippery mud, the streamway's trench;

its scoured, vaulted, array of acoustics.

iii

I hear a figure without eyes or ears.
Follow me, it says.
But I want to go back. I want the warmth
of seeing a child asleep. I want the warmth of a light.
A cup of tea or coffee in sunlight. The sound-cloth of birds.

The cave's mouth smells of the woods'
strange transitional threshold complex.

[*Torch on*.
Torch off.]

It is not far away.

HOB-NAILED BOOT RELEASED
FROM SILTS IN THE UPPER
MELLS STREAM

This boot. Remnant.

Limited, prolonged existence of leather:
stiff tongue; the laminates of a sole
a hundred years out of use.

Risen from the same river into which it was thrown.

Hobnailed parts of the riverbed
migrating through silts.

Whatever future it brings
it is here, now;

having borne through the weeds and waters
its obsolescence.

Through darkness damaged by transparence:
the boots, also,
of children.

They wash down from coal pits upstream:
Moon Pit
Coal Barton
Ringing Bell Mines;

an equanimity of surviving stasis.

What does it mean
to arrive so wretched?

SHATTER CAVE

Nothing has come here
that is more than flicker,
that has not brought
the bright, hurt language of its sun.

Nothing has come here
that is more than flicker,
that has not brought
the bright, hurt language of its sun.

Nothing has come here
that is more than flicker,
that has not brought
the bright, hurt language of its sun.

GREBE SWALLET LEAD MINE

Blackmoor, from lead mining:
straight down into black stal, black ooze.
All that remains now is the flues;
the troubled landscape of hollows.

Beach of black glass, black slag;
black knapweed, yarrow, black roots;
dipped plant; mineral clutter
descending along limestone.

I go in, below,
in rough clothes of soil;
leave cries in the woods;
to go

in, through the percolating leanness of light,
into blackest earth.
A slight wind chafes at the cave mouth.
Unnatural landscape, unnatural airs.

To stop, to listen, from the gaunt cleft,
the buried fissure.

Handprints of children are pressed in the clay
of Grebe Swallet Lead Mine.

The radar bleeps in at me;
birds vaporise out of earshot:

stal. collective (colloquial) term for chemically precipitated mineral deposits
usually of calcite and found in caves – including stalactites, stalagmites, straws,
helictites etc.

crooing pigeons above
harebell above
clinker above
heavy air above.

SLUDGE PIT HOLE
AT GROUND LEVEL

Dry day on the plateau when everything is very dry.
Words have no consciousness.
The river drills towards its ascensions.

ADDRESSING A SMALL PIECE OF VITREOUS SLAG WHICH GIVES OFF A FEELING, CHARTERHOUSE LEAD WORKS

The road here is of black glass: still, heavy with weight.

We are sloping down, now, into the drag of cold.

Slag heap, shifting and stressed; in chinked, obsidian likeness.

What is your name? Who are you? What is your sound?

This could be a woman's glass cup [*picking it up*],
the wine of her sanctuary.
I will drink this moment down into my own black path,
through black rubble and so on, into the thin crack of a room.

One figure to the other bows its head;
delves into the other's dim reflection.

She has gone now, into my plane of vision,
which is like half a black leaf of glass.

Now your turn, as I anchor my cup
with the weight of slag; the leaden, slight glimmer.

And so the other – you with your just-oozed glass arms –
takes and drinks. [*Door slam judder.*]

This is our aven: a gap between huge blocks,
a mutual lost voice going down like bodies into the very deep.
[*Remnants of echoes.*]

I hold the cast of a throat,
a sort of vitreous glass made of a gulp.

aven: a vertical or highly inclined shaft in limestone, extending upward from a
cave passage, generally towards the surface.

ARCHAEOLOGY BENCHWORK:
CALLING THE BARROW NEAR
COAL PIT LANE TO SIGNAL

I have come searching.
I have come looking for your bone, your provenance.
I have come looking.

Today: scours of surface.

What I look for does not reveal more than horizons,
grim lines;
beautifully etch-scoured light searing above shadows.

All feels inconsequential:
this ladybird staggering at low volume into crumbs;
this grass shadow beached on dust.

I know no silence like the stone –
it seeps inside its volume;
cuboid, black voids of rock.

What I search for is the memory and oblivion
of what I search for;

a mineral emotion,
bound in with what is bound in.

You in your grave-layers;
not suffering
but very steadily introverted.

Like you, I am in a room starved of light,
closer to fury;
starved like the collapsed stoup of your throat;
waiting for effort to be superseded,
grace to be given.

Sometimes, it is the dead of night:
but no night exists; nothing disturbs me.

Absence, I miss it: we have no absence.

THE MENDIP (FROM THE OLD FROME ROAD NR WINDWHISTLE) OR A DIAGRAMMATIC EXPERIENCE OF THE MENDIP AS A STAGE FOR ACTS OF WRITING, DRAWN IN THE 3 DIMENSIONS

This is a wide theatre,
thirty miles long.

It dips down at one end
and I can visualise its boreholes
like cast-moulds for bronzes,
scattered at points quite buried.

Some dead, some are empty.
Compressed under the great weight
of everything subsequent;
some tipped out, some are capped:
property devoid of presence.

A man has gone into it.
It's getting late.
I'm conscious of his not returning.

Then, an altering of sequence:

perhaps he has returned,
perhaps I had nodded off.

Maybe I should go out
and call into the blackness;
which means to dig out

into the pressure-space of earth,
which is like heavy fog:
rock's slow liquid of ancient process.

Or maybe I should go to bed,
keep warm;
for the rescue, tomorrow.

GOUGH'S CAVE INHABITANT

Gough's cave, pieces of skull.
I hold that mental
image to the socket of me.
Dark cave of the mouth goes, O.

Come closer, in:
the wild v of its jaw,
the thin clue of its destiny
touched and broken;

tool, unknown of.

But hazard guesses;
hazard knowing what it would have come to
below this nation.
Come deeper, come;

eating on or off the spectrum;
knowing the nook-holes of human flesh,
the bearing of flavour.

What is an animal like,
your own kind, when eaten?

Chewing deeper than England,
eating kindred.
Yellowed bones, all pieces of a ruined past;
the trauma, close.

Did the eater procreate;
sowing the event as a wild signal
in the sequence of blood?

Does that signal possess the present,
its tyrannical energy
persist through the new-born,
and new-born, bearing its memory?

Before ambulance wailings,
before war sirens,
there was the wind, the stampede of a herd;
a theatre of ancestry and of eating.

But this is not England, under England.

In black running water, I hear a sound,
a tongue, going down
into the spatula of fathoms.

Its dark word is a mile of unlit river;
where I hear the craving, gnawing
for meaning at the first sump
where all the dead taint the water.

A mouth of sound, all of its teeth
clamping the kilos of the head.

ANATOMY OF WORMS AS
CONTENT OF SOIL

Once, I discovered a gold locket
  two foot down;
gleamed,
  it flashed as I brought it up.

Opened, it showed two locks of hair;
  one black, one blonde;
then, horsetail, two foot down,
  black roots creeping everywhere;

no use digging to weed it,
  well below topsoil,
right in with the rocks,
  the seizured turmoil of tumbling sludge.

Mice, too,
  working underground
to eat seeds, roots,
  to get their meat below the leaves as they live.

A worm, once, totally knotted,
  a ball of it.
Then binary coins, their two faces
  dull and Britannic,

and there: a femur,
a rib, yellowed, decayed;
a jet bead engraved with an ear of corn;
a clay pipe;

the transitory drawing
of my fingers' clutch,
the small digger, the claw
of the hand, its principle.

ENTERING SOIL AS RAINWATER
AT PRIDDY NINE MAIDENS

The lumps of a spine.
An invested persistence; I can feel it being slow,
barrow to barrow,

the rain's seepage, the foot's threat –
shaking the turf.

The last, unkempt piece of the cemetery weighs
of the very edge.

The ground a swab
of very old hair at the back of a head;
vegetation, rough.

Having been cut, dug, filled-in,
the ground has been cut again.

The brain scooped out:
it no longer asks, it dreams in ash.

The ash in beakers inside the barrows.
Bones, loved or not.

The bones have been longitudinally split.
Twenty miles that way the bones have been longitudinally split.

The battering of all nerves
stands in rainfall.
Waters travel to Stoke Lane Slocker.
Worms aerate their life in the field's surface.

Stones slicken,
a spooned pool rises from the sump.

SINGING RIVER MINE

Into the percolating leanness of light,
into blackest earth.
A slight wind chafes at the cave mouth.

Into the percolating leanness of light,
into blackest earth.
A slight wind chafes at the cave mouth.

Into the percolating leanness of light,
into blackest earth.
A slight wind chafes at the cave mouth.

RUSSIAN COLD WAR MAPS EXAMINED
IN CAMBRIDGE UNIVERSITY LIBRARY
MAP ROOM & REMEMBERED FROM
A SMALL WIDE-MOUTHED CAVE
LOOKING EAST AT BENTER.
(PERSONALLY-NAMED CAVE 'MOON'S
CAVE' FOR ITS POCK-MARKED
SATELLITE-DISH-LIKE RECESS. ONLY
SLIGHT MOON-SIGHTING POSSIBLE,
HOWEVER, DUE TO NORTHWESTERLY
ORIENTATION OF ITS MOUTH.)

Map M-32 . . . Concentric circles
into a time-field of silent devastation;
of fear-infiltrated pages.

In the early '80s
we feared all life's annihilation:

a devotional fear, it kept us subdued.

Localities displaced into Cyrillic versions.
A Russian Radstock: the local town.

Names transposed into threatening effect;
alien intelligence.

The blackbird was not on map M-32,
on a December morning in '79
crouched on the road with a broken wing.

The bulbs of bluebells in earth under moss
were all unmarked.

Skeletal roads, shadows of isolate holdings
present in the invisible.

Telegraph wires tapped for intelligence,
showed no low trembling
ail through poles of bituminised wood.

No badger sett, or roosts of snails
on eroding stone
along the scarp of the west side of the upper valley.

The map indicated
which bridge was built well, which road had capacity.

No fog was marked
straying over thin limestone soils;

no isotopes stained,
raining into makeshift bunkers
under kitchen tables;
deep under eyelids, deep into bloodstreams.

No points were marked
of a Nuclear Winter:

a snow
so invisibly attached to falling;

the luminous, forensic,
soft grey glow of each cold death.

Who was being killed?

On this map:
we in our shelters, under its parallel.

LIMESTONE QUARRY BLASTING
SIREN UNDER FRAIL SUNLIGHT

The quarry siren, a high-pitched *caoine*:
stretched and explicit, it enters the head.

Eclipsing near to song, air minced to death.

Its somnambulant warning
urges us: go in; take shelter. Be scarce.

War-time London does not feel very far;
the nervous fatigue of sheltering figures
feels not very far.

Names of people fall with the quarry rock,
gathering a woollen dust about their moisture.

caoine: Irish spelling of keen, as in keening, lamentation, passionate expression
of grief or sorrow.

REMEMBERING PLUTO'S BATH TUB IN THE WELSH CAVE O.F.D. WHILST AT TWIN POTS IN SWILDON'S HOLE

A river inside the cave up to heart-height.
Eels beat inside it the blackness of unlit blood.

Veins flighting the mass of the body
shiver through to the brain's congenital weight.

No feet, but dissolving tread,
dimming you to very little.
A remote possible phase in love with being;

an extra in the world's underworld, losing sense of the scene.

Earth's daylight, night-time; its flux,
washing off the turn of sun and its leak of moon.

Washing the powerful series of dark and lit caverns
to a scalloping noise
which, after the light has drained down its battery,
continues and just continues

VOICE OF REX LADD, MINING
SURVEYOR (AS THE HOLOGRAM TO
ALL VOICES, ALL ORAL HISTORIES
IN THE DARKNESS OF COAL MINES)
RECORDED AT THE HOUSE HIS
FATHER, COAL HAULIER, BUILT

Your voice, a penumbra
far under the place of your parents' grave.

A scarred pit language;
a spanning, lignite, bituminous speech.

Formidable, used fields.

You love those pits: their gated roads
under the rough, pale, stubborn grasses
on limey clays around Norton Radstock.

Complicated earth.

A fuliginous, filthy, low-bitumen flame
burns
equatorial fragments of an etymology.

Labouring, concealed;
sonorously far-down un-vocalised errors.

Furies who do not decompose
but interact, as bodies matting.

A gas–mineral–fossil.
Soot's unwinding of nuisance intensity:

the petulant, silent vowel that blackened Bristol.

46

Breathing through consonant clinker;
life's shapes laid into its chances;

a staved-in energy crying on all fours,
Oh, mother, if you could only see my poor body now —

forests compressed
to twice the unit of power of wood per cubic inch.

Tree-stumps
metamorphosed at right angles to the gallery:

slicken-sided, illogical
quantities unappeased in the danger of work.
Nothing
like the darkness of coalmines:
it literally presses the eyes;

the lift cage drops
to a buried childhood.

COLD WAR BUNKER, HARPTREE
(DECOMMISSIONED)

A day stretched open by the east wind.
Under field grass: a hatch

I lift

to descend into light-loss; electric,
battery-powered torch.
The room of a bunker, buried.
Its spare existence, an alter-concern.

Miles of all-seeing wind blow at its hollow.

I was a child, I report.
Our dreams were a dim
battle-line of dying flashlight
on the inner retina.

Miles of all-seeing wind blow at its hollow.

As children, we lived vicariously,
but paranoid, anxious, perforated
by a clocked immensity of seeping war.

I see the horizons,
then and here, palpable and steely;
deeper than the scan of visible fields;
periscoped distance; missing routine;

a clocked immensity of seeping war.

I lift up corpses of the ideas of people
manning the gravity of this outpost:
its world committed to dutiful shade.

I hear ventilated air;
air of a long story.

The hatch is peeling;
locked, it stays shut.

But air can enter:
air of a long story,

the constant, radioactive, image of fallout.

SUMP I

Under weights of oblivion,
along tunnels of streams, trickles,
in the blood-soaked iron taste
I will drink when I am cold.

Under weights of oblivion,
along tunnels of streams, trickles,
in the blood-soaked iron taste
I will drink when I am cold.

Under weights of oblivion,
along tunnels of streams, trickles,
in the blood-soaked iron taste
I will drink when I am cold.

MONOLOGUE IN DEEP THRESHOLD, COCKLE'S FISSURE

What is obvious in the dark;
the tragedy, from *tragedian*, the song, the story.

But to tell no story: if I had no story to tell
I would come here like a blind object;
wait, and be told, you must have a story. But I have no story.

The wind is invisible, air is black.
I have this dark (abiding)
of day ungoverned by daylight.

The body slips off-key; its centre is gravity only;
only the effort of negation.

If you were here, with me,
you would also need a place;
somewhere beside a bed you could sit at,
a small high window you could set ajar,
to hear,
because the time of day and of night
have nothing visible
of what you are dispossessed of.

You would not see the leaves
blown out of winter;
nor the palisade of the frosty sun
but the slow step to be taken down
by a leading hand,
to lose autonomy in this black;
however you denote a presence;
to return to the haven which does not exist;
of matted earth, and entrails, and fissures.

The black river of your feet
will retain its conviction;
the story arouse its suffering.

So you would lean, like me,
before a blind reflection;
say,
I am that, in the pool, where there is a crevice.
I am this, flowing into the crevice.

Which you cannot enter,
unless remembering conducts you back –

a long road; agony of cars glinting in sun –
to what is unlit, moving through traffic,
under the siren of the ambulance.

DESCENT INTO
ST CUTHBERT'S SWALLET

At border
psychosis;
void
to assimilate
the body;
a dimmer-switch
fade to
entombing ends;
a violence of
frailty;
to drop
through its rift;
scar-tissue stone;
cold areas of
the body
fall; and on;
crawl
into Pillar
Chamber;
two
visceral forms
fusing forever;
water
like worms.
On. Into Boulder
Chamber;
the hiss
of breath;
the problem
of carbon
dioxide —
heart

beating harder.
A psyche of air-
space; of voice
turning back
to whisper
at an angle,
into the fissure:
Is that you,
Oedipus,
search-lighting
your own
atomised
breath?
By the sound
of a voice
I see.
A song
of droplets
hissed apart:
spores of song
at the entrance
to Harem
Passage,
a black tent
of shade
over stone.
And on,
into Rabbit
Warren,
smooth
with wild clay
and complex:
a hole at foot-
level,
a dripping harp.
Downfault,

downrock;
consolidated
debris,
raking
blackness;
scratches
of movement;
under fossils
through
centuries;
a lifeline
in parallel.
A spotbeam
mirrors
an amber of
halogen;
gold, none,
a gleam;
slight; mineral
staining
a tempering
peculiarity;
fields
of infill.
There is
nowhere
quite like this
river
without sky;
rain-memory
cataracting
calcite, foetal
stalactites,
swelling
to glint;
straws

of crystal,
enfeebled
but wilful,
slowly.
Cascade.
Take a bold step,
or an unwise
step,
crawl
through the
pressure
of tonnes
of rock.
A crashing
white
rig of water;
rope kinked
at the neck;
hanging mid-air;
lucky. On,
into Upper
Traverse
Chamber
through white
noise falling
off
every facet;
dramatised,
a head-swung
light-beam
at low wattage;
radiance
continuously
dimming;
a vague arena
that

echoes through
vapours
siphoned off
into the lobes
of the eyes,
into deeper
looms,
bearing fathoms.
Skull
with no sockets.
The voice
booms. On.
If I am to be
blind;
what does it
mean?
It means,
down here in this
dark it is hard
to explain
in the words
of daylight
exactly
what is meant
in the dark.
The guide is low
on energy reserve –
who
due to coldness,
strenuous
descent,
drop-verticals
to cling to,
cannot commit.
He's diabetic,
this is a three-

Mars Bar trip,
he's only
brought two.
And Stal Pitch is
difficult.
Shining beads
on the
underneaths
of mineries
above,
false floors;
loose-packed.
Rocks of
smooth
irregularity;
sinking holes
of draught;
undermined,
thin
skeletal bits
of riverbed;
a static-
hammock
for water;
cat's cradle
of stalagmite;
stashed-up
sediment.
On. Into Railway
Tunnel,
for obvious
reasons,
long, half-
cylindrical,
terminal;
freighted

with
intermission.
To slither
down clay-slip
thinking
in the crease-
noise
of wet-proof
gear
at the fault's
45 degree
decline.
What is this life?
Odd-ball
mud formations
like clusters of
grapes:
the Tideline
of Bacchus
330 feet
under the rough
grounds of
Priddy's
lead works.
On. Into Stal
Pitch Bypass;
stream crystal,
pinnacles
of glint;
bones inside
hands grip
bones inside
arms,
water of cold,
over the beams
of the back;

coiled wires
of network,
gour pool scum
radically
in-growing its
slow skin
soap flakes
into the three
dimensions.
Cave pearls
spun, too,
out of calcite-
rich waters.
Relic
of inhaled, effigy
of exhaled
breath,
to a wedge,
thinning
into a lung-like
chasm.
On,
into Stafford's
Boulder
Problem,
the bloom of
condensation;
milk-bluish
airs.
A stripped-down
means

gour: flowstone deposit, normally of calcite, built up along the edge of a pool
due to precipitation for a thin film of overflow water. Gour pools are usually
small pools which form from such precipitation and deposit, also known as rim-
stone dams.

of survival,
to return
at all costs;
under twisting
hairs of stone
and its havocs,
ascend
by blind
foot–hole,
levering
against a back
wall to brake;
where the
minery stream
falls;
cold black
poisoned
water;
when the light
goes out.

SOIL & SUBSOIL, COCKLE'S FIELD

What did I dig for, which are not the dreams I will get?

I am so cold
I have to dig the sodden staining of a century,
and the black felt of twenty dialects
which are dead only in upper spaces.

Here, they still thrive:
small, congesting bodies in organic silt
many would have dredged for a second coming.

I cannot adhere to the surface-country,
but will go into blacker reaches of area;
attempting illumination of another order,
without geography.

Under the weight of oblivion;
along tunnels of streams, trickles,
in the blood-soaked iron taste
I will drink when I am cold; without myself.

Will not feel the frost freezing my hair stiff
but be below the frost's liturgy of scrap-metal,
its water-shrapnel.

Will loiter nameless, waiting
for the hole to absorb me.

Bury me, I will say,
with my fish skeleton eyes, my wasting jaws,
my cold patience, prevalent, losing the battle;
by the black pond beyond the pond edge.

Below the porous swarming of matter,
under the frog's gelatinous clotting of its eggs;
which is all an eye, and another eye
staring inwardly, where there is no light —

will contrive to be lifeless;
under dead leaf, root-shake,
under creatures pausing in earth to hear.

Or be like the mole: anti-social
in sinews of machinery digging depths under fur;

where all is shallow,
where all is deep too.